PILGRIM

OF THE

CLOUDS

PILGRIM OF THE CLOUDS

POEMS AND ESSAYS FROM MING CHINA

by Yüan Hung-tao
translated by
Jonathan Chaves

WEATHERHILL
New York · Tokyo

Some of the poems in this collection have appeared in *Montemora, The Virginia Quarterly Review,* and *First Issue.*

First edition, 1978
Inklings edition, 1992

Published by Weatherhill, Inc., 420 Madison Avenue, 15th Floor, New York, NY 10017. Protected by copyright under terms of the International Copyright Union; all rights reserved. Except for fair use in book reviews, no part of this book may be reproduced for any reason by any means, including any method of photographic reproduction, without permission of the publisher. Printed in the United States.

Library of Congress Cataloging in Publication Data

Yüan, Hung-tao, 1568–1610.
     Pilgrim of the clouds: poems and essays from Ming China / by Yuan Hung-tao; translated by Jonathan Chaves.
     p.   cm.
Translated from Chinese.
ISBN 0-8348-0257-0
     1. Yuan, Hung-tao, 1568–1610—Translations into English.
I. Chaves, Jonathan.   II. Title.
PL2698.Y85A24   1992
895.1'8409—dc20

92-19892
CIP

FOR ANNA, MY WIFE

"As long as the sky . . . "

CONTENTS

ACKNOWLEDGMENTS

I must thank members of the Chinese Poetry Discussion Group, particularly Nathan Sivin, Hung Ming-shui, and Kao Yu-kung. To Irving Lo goes the credit for first calling my attention to the riches of Ming poetry.

My wife, Anna Caraveli Chaves, to whom this is dedicated, is a gifted translator of Greek poetry. She has helped iron out several infelicities of expression. But it is her unflagging moral support for which I am especially grateful.

INTRODUCTION

Yüan Hung-tao (1568–1610) was one of the major poets and essayists of the Ming dynasty, a period that has been described as both the culmination of China's traditions and the source of subsequent developments in China. Yüan's short life (he died at the age of forty-two) falls within the "late Ming," a period of political decadence and confusion but also a time of brilliance in the arts.

The political and social turmoil that marked these decades is epitomized by the arrogant cruelty of the eunuch Wei Chung-hsien (1568–1627). Born in the same year as Yüan Hung-tao, Wei eventually became a favorite of the governess to the incompetent emperor Hsi Tsung (r. 1620–27). Exercising almost total power, Wei destroyed his enemies ruthlessly until sent into exile himself, whereupon he committed suicide. His corpse was dismembered by imperial decree, the ultimate degradation in Confucian society.

While the world of the literati was being shaken by the corruption of political power, various complex factors led to the numerous peasant rebellions that also characterized the late Ming. Nor were the sufferings of the scholar-officials and those of the Chinese masses completely unrelated. For example, there was a remarkable demonstration in Suchou against the arrest of a respected official by the agents of Wei Chung-hsien in which both literati and thousands of commoners took part.

A period of deep social problems often becomes a time of intense intellectual, religious, and artistic activity. The late Ming was unquestionably such a period. Both painting and art historical theory were innovative. Yüan Hung-tao was a friend of Tung Ch'i-ch'ang (1555–1636), the leading art theorist. After conversing with Tung, Yüan was moved to reflect: "The good painter learns from things, not from other painters. The good philosopher learns from his mind, not from some doctrine. The good poet learns from the panoply of images, not from writers of the past." Yüan saw a basic principle of individualism underlying creativity in all fields.

Late-Ming philosophy was characterized by the revival of Buddhism, along with the continuing popularity of the School of Wang Yang-ming in Neo-Confucian thought. Wang Yang-ming (1472–1529) represents an emphasis on the individual mind as opposed to social norms. Wang felt that within each person there is an essentially good "intuitive awareness" (liang-chih) in which we can all trust. This concept derived ultimately from the classical philosopher Mencius, but it undoubtedly owed a great deal to Buddhist influence as well, especially the notion that each individual has the "Buddha-nature" within and need only become aware of it. For the school of Wang Yang-ming to triumph in the late Ming was for individualism to replace extreme allegiance to tradition in Chinese intellectual life.

This is not to deny the continued presence of those who were outraged by what they considered the excessive individualism of some of Wang Yang-ming's later followers. In their view, the most offensive of these was Li Chih (1527–1602). Li called for reliance on one's own intuitions and desires, which he associated with what he called the "childlike mind." He was, not surprisingly, one of Yüan Hung-tao's friends. Li eventually shaved his head and became an unordained Buddhist monk. He so incensed his more conservative contemporaries that in 1602 he was arrested and his writings burned. In jail, Li committed suicide by cutting his throat.

In this highly charged environment, Buddhism played an important role. The leading Buddhist was the monk Chu-hung (1535–1615), whose great achievement was the unification of Ch'an Buddhism, oriented toward the practice of meditation leading to revelation of one's innate Buddha-nature, and Pure Land Buddhism, which was devotional and called for repetition of the name of Amitabha, the Buddha of the Western Paradise ("Pure Land"), where the devotee would hope to gain rebirth. Chu-hung argued that the mind is in fact the Pure Land, without denying the reality of the Pure Land. In other words, he brought together the intellectual, meditative, and devotional tendencies in Buddhism that had previously developed more or less separately. Chu-hung even debated with one of the first Jesuit missionaries to China, Matteo Ricci. (Yüan Hung-tao also knew Ricci, who died in Peking in 1610, the same year as Yüan.) Ricci opposed the Buddhist concept of rebirth and was also against the vegetarianism that Chu-hung championed. He expressed the Christian position that man is the "crown of creation," and that animals were intended for man's benefit.

Chu-hung instructed Yüan Hung-tao and his brothers in Buddhist thought and practice. They and their friends organized "Clubs for Releasing Life," in which the members would recite Amitabha's name, make offerings, discuss the sutras, and purchase live animals from butchers and then set them free, thus gaining merit.

No matter which aspect of late Ming intellectual life we have discussed—Buddhism, the Wang Yang-ming branch of Neo-Confucianism, or painting and art theory—we have found that Yüan Hung-tao was a friend of the central figure involved: Chu-hung, Li Chih, and Tung Ch'i-ch'ang.

Poetry and poetic theory prior to the time of Yüan Hung-tao were dominated by orthodox archaism, which glorified eighth-century T'ang poetry. Poets such as Tu Fu and Li Po were thought to represent perfection, and a writer of the present age need only emulate their styles. Needless to say, this view was anathema to Yüan Hung-tao, his elder brother Tsung-tao (1560–1600), and their younger brother Chung-tao (1570–1624), who together constituted what came to be known as the Kung-an school (after Kung-an Subprefecture, their ancestral home). The Kung-an school advocated direct expression of emotion and individuality.

Yüan felt strongly that the movement to "restore the past" (fu-ku) was misguided. He believed that, "as the ways of society undergo change, literature must follow suit." In a letter to a close friend, Yüan wrote: "In general, things are prized when they are authentic. If I am to be authentic, then my face cannot be the same as your face, and how much less the face of some man of antiquity!"

In another letter, Yüan writes that "the greatness of the T'ang poets lay in their refusal to model themselves on others." Yüan's use of the term *wu-fa* ("no style") looks ahead to the famous paradoxical formulation by the Ch'ing painter Shih-t'ao (1642–1707): "The method which consists in following no method is the perfect method." Obviously, neither Yüan nor

Shih-t'ao is calling for lack of discipline or chaos in art. The point is rather that one should follow one's inner feelings, or "native sensibility" (*hsing-ling*), rather than some external authority. There is a clear parallel to Wang Yang-ming's emphasis on "intuitive awareness."

Yüan Hung-tao's view of literature led him, as might be expected, to find literary value in unusual places. While he certainly admired many of the established poets, Yüan shared with Li Chih and the remarkable critic Chin Sheng-t'an (d. 1661) the opinion that fiction, drama, and even folk songs must be seen as serious literature as well. In traditional China, novels and plays were barely tolerated as entertainment; they certainly did not qualify as high art, on the same level with classical poetry, essays, and historical writing. And folk songs were almost totally neglected.

But Yüan Hung-tao was a friend and admirer of one of the leading Ming playwrights, T'ang Hsien-tsu (1550–1616), and in a list of his own favorite reading, Yüan casually mentions the great novel *Shui-hu chuan* (*Water Margin*, translated by Pearl Buck as *All Men Are Brothers*) and the plays of the Yüan dynasty (the golden age of Chinese drama) side by side with the poetry of Tu Fu and *Records of the Historian* by Ssu-ma Ch'ien, China's most respected historian.

Most contemporary writing will not endure, Yüan says, because it is blindly imitative of earlier works. But the songs sung by village women and children are a different matter:

> These are composed by real people, so they have real resonance! They are not slavish imitations of the Han and Wei dynasties; they do not follow in the footsteps of the High T'ang period. They are

produced naturally, from the inner nature, and they express human happiness, anger, grief, joy, love, and desire. This is what makes them worth savoring.

Yüan also recognized the artistry of the Chinese shadow-puppet theater, a form of popular theater widely disseminated and still performed in countries such as Indonesia, Thailand, Turkey, and Greece. He was inspired to write a group of three poems on the subject, in one of which he says:

> They may not have bones or sinews,
> but they have spirit!

Yüan obtained his *chin-shih* degree in 1592, which enabled him to enter the official bureaucracy. While performing the duties of magistrate of Wu-hsien (Suchou), he wrote to his friends:

It's not that I'm unwilling to be an official, but I can't help feeling that it simply runs against the grain of my heart! . . . superiors visit you like gathering clouds, travelers stop by like drops of rain, papers pile up like mountains, an ocean of taxes in cash or grain must be collected: if you work and write morning and night, you still can't keep up with all of it!

Far more interesting to Yüan were the literary gatherings of the Grape Society (P'u-t'ao she) that he and his brothers founded at the Ch'ung-kuo Temple of Peking in 1598; his Buddhist activities, centering around the monk Chu-hung; and, perhaps most important of all, the many journeys he made to the magnificent mountains of China. These journeys inspired Yüan's superb travel essays. It is clear from his essays that he often went beyond the paths to clamber up cliff faces or to crawl through caves. Yüan was searching for new experiences in nature, partly in the hope that these would breathe new life into his poetry.

Yüan Hung-tao has been remembered less for his poetry than for his other achievements. Yüan's literary theory (shared by his brothers) is so striking that there is a tendency to discuss the philosophy of the Kung-an school and ignore the poetry itself. But a careful reading of Yüan's poetry reveals him to be the single greatest poet of the Ming dynasty, more inventive even than Kao Ch'i (1336–74), to whom this title would be granted by most.

Despite his polemics against imitation of the past, Yüan was not afraid to write on traditional themes. But he did so in such a way as to apply these themes to his own expressive needs. For example, the poem

"Twenty-first Day of the Seventh Month" (pp. 82–83) draws heavily on the rich imagery and impressionistic atmosphere of innumerable poems on the ancient "neglected wife" theme, as well as on the elegiac tone of laments for the dead (*tao-wang*), but Yüan leaves his sources far behind. Not only does the poem appear to modulate from the third person to the first person of the man (rather than the woman, as was traditional), but the gentle melancholy of the neglected-wife poems gives way to real passion. This passion is not expressed explicitly, but rather through an almost surreal use of imagery and the kinds of imaginative leaps—between past and present, concrete and abstract, waking and dreaming—that one expects of a Lorca or a Neruda. The last four lines of the poem are a triumphant synthesis of all these levels.

Similarly, in "Making Fun of Myself on People Day" (pp. 35–36), the poet purposely takes upon himself every available stereotyped role in Chinese literati society, while avoiding precisely the actions most characteristic of those roles. He is an official who does not wear official robes, a farmer who does not plow his fields, a Confucian scholar who does not read books, a Taoist hermit who delights in sensuality. The idea is developed in increasingly exciting imagery of liberation, until two classical allusions bring the poem back down to earth.

Yüan wrote a number of poems in which the everyday lives of the common people he so admired are beautifully evoked. He creates as rich a tapestry as the storytellers who produced *Shui-hu chuan* and other early novels:

The boatwoman . . .
Her left hand steadies a little girl,
    her right works the rudder . . .

A little boy runs out into the road,
    blocks the way, and shouts:
    "I am the King of the Bull Fights!"

In his prose writings too, Yüan creates vignettes of life in realms of society that were rarely depicted in classical Chinese literature. A letter to one of his uncles offers a rare glimpse of living conditions among the urban poor:

Tsung Ping [375–443] has said: "I have found that riches are not as good as poverty and high position not as good as low." I used to think this was a pretentious statement. But now I believe it. . . . Just look in the old temples and cold shops along the streets of Ch'ang-an at midnight: there the beggar boys and mendicant monks are snoring away like thunder. Meanwhile, the white-haired old millionaires are huddled among their silken blankets, behind their bed curtains, wishing in vain for just a moment of shut-eye!

Yūan's poems and essays (which can be regarded as prose poems of a sort) continue to retain the liveliness and expressiveness that set them apart three hundred and fifty years ago from the dry, academic exercises of many of his contemporaries.

POEMS BY
YÜAN HUNG-TAO

Chang Jui-t'u: "Two Men Gazing at a Waterfall." *Detail from hanging scroll, ink on silk, 120 x 52.2 cm. Collection unknown.*

LEAVING Po-Hsiang at Dawn

I get out of bed before sunrise
and, half asleep, climb into my carriage.
These official journeys are like food stuck in the teeth,
homesickness as unpalatable as spoiled
      water chestnuts!
A girl stands in front of an inn, her hair uncombed.
A Buddhist monk boils water in a little hut.
Not intoxicated, but not sober either,
I listen as the morning drum sounds through the dust.

ON RECEIVING News of My Termination

The time has come to devote myself to my
    hiker's stick;
I must have been a Buddhist monk in a former life!
Sick, I see returning home a kind of pardon.
A stranger here—being fired is like being promoted.
In my cup, thick wine; I get crazy-drunk,
eat my fill, then stagger up the green mountain.
The southern sect, the northern sect, I've tried
    them all:
this hermit has his own school of Zen philosophy.

A PLAYFUL POEM on Seeing a Rubbing of Some of
My Poetry at Ting-chou

In the pagoda—an ink rubbing of my verses!
Whoever engraved them here?
They fill the air, like the chirping of a worm;
cover the wall—calligraphy like insects!
Sooner or later, they'll be eaten away by the moss
or effaced by the wind and rain.
But for now, my poems have been cut in stone:
my seal-vermilion drips to the ground below.

*The rubbing would be made from a stone engraving. Paper
would be placed over the stone, and ink pressed carefully against
the paper. A seal might be applied, using vermilion ink.*

ON MEETING MY ELDER BROTHER Upon Arriving
in the Capital—A Poem on His Recent Life

You have turned your back on the busy crowds of the
    world and chant to yourself from secondhand
    books.
Your official post is not important—
you have few contacts with people;
a long stay in the capital has brought new wrinkles
    to your face.
On the cracked walls are portraits of Buddhist monks;
high in the windows, birds' nests can be seen.
Editor at the Academy—not the greatest job,
but still, be careful of the wind and waves!

MAKING FUN of Myself on "People Day"
Seventh day of the first month.

This official wears no official sash,
this farmer pushes no plow,
this Confucian does not read books,
this recluse does not live in the wilds.
In society, he wears lotus leaves for clothes,
among commoners, he is decked out in cap and jade.
His serenity is achieved without closing the door,
his teaching is done without instruction.
This Buddhist monk has long hair and whiskers,
this Taoist immortal makes love to beautiful women.
One moment, withering away in a silent forest,
the next, bustling through crowds on city streets.
When he sees flowers, he calls for singing girls;
when he has wine to drink, he calls for a pair of dice.

His body is as light as a cloud
floating above the Great Clod.
Try asking the bird, flying in the air:
"What clear pond reflects your image?"
How free! the dragon, curling, leaping,
liberated! beyond this world, or in it.
The official, Liu-hsia Hui, firm, yet harmonious;
or Hermit Yi, pure in his retirement.

RISING FROM MY SICKBED, I Saw the Moon as the Sky Cleared

This was the night of the midautumn moon of the year i-ssu [1605].

Up from my sickbed, I meet the full moon—

the clouds open, a smile opens on my face.

The clouds depart with what's left of my depression;

the moon appears with the new good feelings.

Falling leaves are iced with clear dew,

new fragrance rises from the thick wine.

This gladness is still not deep in my heart,

but these are embers, ready to burst into flame.

DREAMING

The dream world cannot be found
    away from my pillow—
but nowhere on the pillow can I find it.
And when I am in the dream world
my pillow might as well not exist.
Awake, I feel my dreams are empty;
in dream, the waking world has disappeared.
Can I be sure that the waking universe
has no pillow beneath it?
If dream and waking alternate,
which is fantasy, which is real?

THE FIRST DAY of Spring—On the Gold Ox Road

This is the day the farmer puts down his plow,
the young girl leaves her loom,
the scholar sets aside his books,
the official stops collecting taxes,
the merchant closes shop,
the fisherman hauls in his nets . . .
So why am I the only man
walking dangerous slopes, under towering
    mountains?

THE "SLOWLY, SLOWLY" POEM
Playfully inscribed on the wall.

The bright moon slowly, slowly rises,
the green mountains slowly, slowly descend.
The flowering branches slowly, slowly redden,
the spring colors slowly, slowly fade.
My salary slowly, slowly increases,
my teeth slowly, slowly fall out,
my lover's waist slowly, slowly expands,
my complexion slowly, slowly ages.

We are low in society
    in the days of our greatest health,
our pleasure comes when we are no longer young.
The Goddess of Good Luck
    and the Dark Lady of Bad Luck

are with us every step we take.

Even heaven and earth are imperfect

and human society is full of ups and downs.

Where do we look for real happiness?

—Bow humbly, and ask the Masters of Taoist Arts.

A RECORD OF MY TRIP to Mount She

1

Yellow leaves spiral down through the air;
waterfall spray flies into raindrops.
Patches of moss darken Buddha's face;
the stones here have been brushed by the robes
    of a god.
The monks are tranquil, though their kitchen has
    few vegetables;
the mountain, cold—not many sparrows in the flock.
Of themselves, my worries all disappear;
I do not have to try to forget the world.

2

Height after height of strange mountain scenes,
new words, new ideas in our conversation.

Wild pines blow in the wind like hanging manes;

the ancient rocks are covered with mottled scales.

I enter the temple, seek the dream world of
    the monks,

thumb through sutras, feel the dustiness of this
    traveler's life.

You, the Zen master, and I, a lover of wine—

we are brothers, way beyond the people of the world.

TRAVELING BY BOAT to Gold Harbor—
Drinking With San-mu and Wang Hui

How happy I feel in the country!
All along the riverbank—flowers on the hedges.
Old farmers sit in the fields, crushing lice;
river girls lie with their fishing poles, asleep.
The households in this little harbor
    pay their taxes in reeds;
the granary holds rice duties
    collected from the barges.
We have a boat and some fresh wine to drink—
this happiness has nothing to do with money!

Lan Ying: "Landscape in the Manner of Wang Meng." *Dated 1640.
Detail from hanging scroll, ink and light colors on paper, 95.5 x 37.8
cm. Art Museum, Princeton University.*

GETTING UP in the Morning After Staying Overnight at Huan-chu Temple

Hey there, Yüan Hung-tao!
Why not get up with the crack of dawn?
A hundred thousand universes
    have been blown by the wind
into an ocean of cloud.
—I throw on my clothes,
    go out and take a look:
sure enough, the clouds are stretched out below.
The whole sky is filled with crystal forms—
such is the power of the mountain god!

I WENT OUT at night with the monk Liao. We
went to Wang's for drinks. When the wine had been
served, a great thunderstorm started up. Everyone
else flinched with fright, but I felt wonderful. The
storm went on until after midnight.

Heaven is in a dark, ugly mood—
rumbling thunder, driving wind and rain.
Books tumble off the desk, into storage jars;
the children run and hide under their beds.
And Master Shan?—He slams his fist on the table,
    shouts out loud,
wets his whistle from a cup of rhinoceros horn
and walks home
    without a candle
flashes of red lightning
    lighting his way.

SAYING GOODBYE to the Monk Wu-nien

Each five years we meet
then grieve when we must part.
It has taken only three farewells
for fifteen years to pass.
I recall how I tried to study meditation with you
but I was like the yellow poplar
    which grows for a while
        then shrinks again.
A hundred times I heard you lecture
but my mind remained a tangled knot.
I was like a man born blind
who has never seen red or purple—
try explaining the difference to him
and the more you speak
    the more confused he'll get.

I can't bear to leave you now
but it is impossible for us
    to stay together.
It is October—the river winds are blowing hard;
please let your hair grow back in
    to protect your head from the cold.

CHRYSANTHEMUMS in Winter

There are no flowers that never fade,
yet here are the chrysanthemums,
    still blooming in winter.
To protect their leaves, I weave a bamboo trellis;
to keep them fragrant, cut away the weeds.
Now, chilling our hearts, the cold breaks upon us;
old friends come, bringing wine.
Suddenly, we remember the old man of the
    eastern hedge,
chant his poems out loud, raise our cups in a toast.

"The old man of the eastern hedge" refers to T'ao Ch'ien (365-427), famous for his love of chrysanthemums. His best-known couplet on the subject is: "I pluck chrysanthemums beneath the eastern hedge, / and, in the distance, see the southern mountains."

POEM WRITTEN at Willow Lake

At sunset, I lie down for a nap—
the mountains seem to tumble onto my pillow.
Green mosses are reflected in the water;
winds from the rice fields blow through the window.
I enjoy myself here, arranging rocks and flowers
    in the garden,
writing out spells to keep away crows and bugs.
My drinking companions are mostly Buddhist monks:
even when we're drunk, we talk about the Void.

This poem is one from a group of three. A friend gave Willow Lake to Yüan Hung-tao in exchange for a Buddhist statue.

Drinking at the Studio of Fang Wei-chin

There are many pleasures to be enjoyed
    at your studio:
we play chess, have a drinking contest . . .
The waters of the Wei lap the walls;
we see the reflections of sailing boats
    in the wine jug.
Fish hawks peer down at your brush rack;
riverside flowers fall among the chessmen.
We roll up a curtain, meet new poems,
chant them out loud as we look
    at the catalpa trees.

I RECENTLY BOUGHT a fancy boat that I plan to
make my home, so I have written a series of poems
on living in a boat.

I plan to make this boat my peaceful home,
under the moon, following the wind
    wherever it may lead.
The fish and waterbirds?
    I'll ask them to be my secretaries.
The clouds and mist will hire me as their scribe.
I'll live here like a wood grub,
    deep within the tree,
and travel like the snail,
    who carries his own home.
Beneath me—not a strip of land;
    above—not one roof tile.
From this day on, I entrust my body
    to the elements.

WRITING DOWN What I See

The setting sun brings a pallor to the face of autumn;
floating clouds gather quickly into clusters.
They slant down, veiling the trees,
only two or three mountains still visible in the haze.
My horse glances back at the bridge-spanned river;
a group of monks returns along a path of pine trees.
The cliff is too high—I can see no temple;
suddenly, through the mist I hear
    a temple bell.

Ch'en Hung-shou: "Solitary Wanderer Beneath Pine." *Album leaf, ink and colors on silk, 31.7 x 24.9 cm. Nanking Museum.*

ON BOARD a Boat at Chi-ning

The mouth of the Wen River—240 feet wide,
a torrent like a cliff of water, all the way across.
In one night, a wind that blows the grain boats
    from the south
has swept us as far as the Nan-wang locks.
How many days since I left my home?
In an instant, months and months have passed!
Traveling by canal, there's been no fixed schedule
but now we should be one stage from Peking.
For a hundred li—a storm of yellow sand
in a dry wind that sounds like ripped cloth.

I've long since been competing for a place at the table;
my body feels sullied by the muddy waves.
Thirty years old, and what have I accomplished?

Strive, strive—for a cluster of empty hopes.
Compare me to a boat, struggling upstream,
which gains one foot, and then loses two.

AT WHITE DEER SPRING

A little fishpond, just over two feet square,
and not terribly deep.
A pair of goldfish swim in it
as freely as if in a lake.
Like bones of mountains among icy autumn clouds
tiny stalagmites pierce the rippling surface.
For the fish, it is a question of being alive—
they don't worry about the depth of the water.

WEST LAKE

One day I walk by the lake.
One day I sit by the lake.
One day I stand by the lake.
One day I lie by the lake.

This poem is one from a set of two.

"SONGS of the Bamboo Branches"

1

At the mouth of the Lung-chou River
    the water looks like sky:
here the women of Lung-chou operate the great boats.
Waves splashing her face, one of them asks the traveler,
"Are you scared? Watch my boat list
    under eight feet of wind!"

2

The boatwoman has painted eyebrows.
Her boat is like a leaf, following the waves of the river.
Her left hand steadies a little girl,
    her right works the rudder,
and her dark hair, piled high as a mountain,
    stays perfectly in place.

AFTER READING Chi-tien's Poems on West Lake

How many times
    have I stepped alone
        into the boat at West Lake?
The boatman knows me now
    and never asks for money.
One note sung by a bird
    breaks the total silence—
it sounds from the mountain
    that slants below
        the setting sun.

This poem is one from a group of four. Chi-tien was possibly Tao-chi (d. 1209), a Buddhist monk of the Sung dynasty.

IMPROVISED on the Road (1)

In the second month I returned to my home town.
In the fourth month—back on the road again.
Children gaze at me in the narrow lanes;
across the steam, a scholar laughs out loud.

This poem is one from a group of three.

IMPROVISED on the Road (2)

He rides a thoroughbred, with bridle of red silk.
He wears an official cap, and a robe
    embroidered with gold dragons.
A little boy runs out into the road,
    blocks the way, and shouts:
"I am the King of the Bull Fights!"

This poem is one from a group of six.

THINGS EXPERIENCED

Green leaves start to wither on the trees;
white waves sweep across the river.
People gossip of invasions in the east;
rumors fly: "We've sent ships from the north!"
I buy some Ch'ü-chou oranges, spotted with frost;
listen all day to famous women singers.
There are many marriage ceremonies here in
    Yang-chou—
flutes and drums play loud as night draws on.

Yoshitaka Iriya considers the third and fourth lines to refer to Hideyoshi's notorious invasion of Korea in 1592; the Chinese did in fact dispatch ships with troops and food to aid the Korean cause.

HSIN-AN RIVER

The waves here are bad
    the head winds are terrible;
the foliage, all green—even the rocks are green.
From dark cliffs we hear
    the murmuring of ghosts,
wild fires wake dragons with their heat.
The trees are old—from T'ang-dynasty stock;
the steles, toppled over,
    bear Sung-dynasty inscriptions.
Stepping ashore, we meet an old farmer
who claims that ape men inhabit these woods.

This poem is one from a group of ten.

ON THE EIGHTEENTH DAY *of the twelfth month, I
arrived at Ch'i-yang and left my boat. From Hsing-kuo I
traveled to Hsien-ning, taking a route that emerged at Gold
Ox Commandery. The mountain road was like the blade of a
knife; whirling snow froze the skin, and the sedan-chair
bearers were so miserable they could hardly walk. But there
were mountains everywhere covered with snow—some like
crows' necks, others like piles of jewels. This is indeed one of
the pleasures of traveling. Along the way, I improvised poems
on the things I saw, and ended up with sixteen quatrains.*

3

Wild bamboo, roots clutching the rocks:
village women, speaking with a trace
    of a southern accent . . .
The guide points ahead and says to me:
"That's Little Fork Mountain up there!"

9

Don't be upset that the horses' hoofs are sinking.
Don't worry because the cart wheels are stuck in
    the mud.
Imagine if you were alone here with your
    walking stick,
trudging through the snow to look at the mountains!

12

Peak after peak, dotted with snow;
bend after bend, cold mountain stream—
I have a feeling of déjà vu;
in a painting by Wang Wei I've seen this place before.

13

A man is walking along a craggy ridge;
his head appears above a cliff, then disappears again.

A horse descends a bridge across a stream
and suddenly is swallowed by the snow.

16
Pigs tied to the throne of the Heavenly King;
birds nesting in the cap of the Great Judge.
Chickens perch here,
    and make a market of their own;
wood from a deer pen forms the gate.

These are five poems from the group of sixteen.

Ch'eng Chia-sui: "Landscape with Figures." *Leaf from an album dated
1639, ink on paper, 23.1 x 12.8 cm. National Palace Museum, Taipei.*

"IN CH'ANG-AN There is a Narrow Road"

She reins in her horse,
stands by the watering trough.
Loquats falling—it is autumn—
    dogwood in bloom.
The girl is from Shansi, a turban on her head,
face heavy with make-up, hair thick with grease.
She plays the zither of twenty-five strings
and wears a gown of scarlet with purple threads.
Smiling, she asks:
    "Is this how they dress down south?"

The title of this poem is the name of a well-known song.

CLIMBING MOUNT YANG

Craggy rocks, crouching like elephants;
withered pine bark, mottled like fish scales.
From which spot did the Crane Immortal take off?
Is the Dragon Mother possessed of real magic power?
The caves here have talking animals;
on the cliffs live people who never say a word.
The palace of Wu fell apart long ago—
where can the ruins be found?

See Yüan's prose essay on Mount Yang, translated on pp. 110–12

CLIMBING MOUNT HUA

At Shan-sun Pavilion, put on the turban
and become a pilgrim who visits the clouds
    and pays his respects to the rocks.
The waters have a secret method
    for flowing beyond this world;
the mountains are like a drug
    for lightening the body.
Before the eyes, Mount Hua—
    a wall of 10,000 feet.
On the robe—a single speck of dust from the city.
If you come across a chessboard, stay for a while:
before you know it, the wildflowers
    will fade
    and bloom again.

*This poem is one from a group of six. According to legend, a poet
once met an immortal near the summit of Mount Hua, and they*

played a game of wei-ch'i chess (Japanese go) that lasted through
several changes of the seasons. A Pavilion for Playing Chess now
stands on this spot.

AT THE SUMMIT of Mount Hua—For My Fellow Traveler the Taoist Shu

You have walked everywhere on the autumn clouds,
    trod the purple moss,
searched for pine trees on the palm
    of the great spirit.
Chang K'ai could conjure up fog
    from his native valley;
Tung-fang Shuo in a former life
    could command the thunder.
You too are a master of Taoist magic,
and you have a sense of humor—
    almost an immortal!

Lotus Peak—a straight drop of 40,000 feet:
only crazy people ever climb this far.

*Chang K'ai of the Latter Han dynasty was said to be able to con-
jure up fog over an area of five square li. Tung-fang Shuo was a
famous wit of the Former Han dynasty.*

Tung Ch'i-ch'ang: "A Buddhist Temple Among Hills by a River,
After Chü-jan." Dated 1630. *Leaf from an album of eight landscapes,
ink on paper, 25 x 16.3 cm. Art Museum, Princeton University.*

TOGETHER WITH CHU FEI-ERH, Wang I-hsü,
and Tuan Hui-chih I stopped at Hsing-chiao Temple
and looked out at the view of South Mountain.

The place is ancient—
    no histories say how old;
the terrace, crumbling—
    don't ask when it was built.
Fragrant winds
    blow across Wei Family Ridge;
brilliant snow-light
    sparkles in Fan Stream.
The country temple, half-hidden
    by red maple leaves;
people's houses, interspersed
    with clumps of blue-green lotus.

Across the stream, the mountains
 are still more beautiful—
we mount our horses,
 gallop into the gray mist.

TRAVELING Through Huai-an by Boat

Three hundred miles along the canal;
ten thousand willow branches, my broken heart.
Travel is the root of sorrow, clings to it like glue;
meditation—that is the way to control this suffering.
Homesick, I think about fish-on-rice;
drunk, I dream about clam chowder . . .
More and more, too lazy to study books,
spider webs covering my brush rack.

PEI-MANG CEMETERY

Old pine trees, their shaggy manes
    twirled in a dance by the wind;
row on row of tombs, one wisp of smoke
    rising from nowhere.
The lords and princes who once lived
    along Bronze Camel Avenue
have become the dust that settles on the traveler's face.
The white poplar on top of the mountain
    has turned into an old woman
who spends each night in the fields,
    chasing away tigers of stone.
Officials come to this place, face north
    toward the Mausoleum of Longevity,
and give thanks that the crows who perch here
    speak Chinese.

ON HEARING That a Girl of the Ts'ui Family Has
Become a Disciple of the Buddhist Master Wu-
nien—Playfully Offered to the Master

She has cut off her conch-shell hairdo,
    thrown away her eyebrow pencil;
the passions have been quenched by a single
    cup of tea.
Her sandalwood clappers now accompany
    Sanskrit chanting;
her silk dress has been recut:
    a makeshift cassock.
The Master's mind is like quiet water
    reflecting this moon.
His body is a cold forest
    putting forth this blossom.
How many times can she remember

the hand of ordination
on her brow?
Generation after generation,
life after life
in the family of Buddha!

Shao Mi: "Landscape with Figure, in the Manner of Wen Cheng-ming." *Leaf from an album, ink and light colors on silk, 29.6 x 21.2 cm. National Palace Museum, Taipei.*

PAYING MY RESPECTS to the Mummy of the Monk Ch'ang-erh

The wheel of samsara has come to a peaceful halt;
the gleam of the lacquered body—
    as fresh as a polished mirror!
I know that his soul has long since vanished,
but—amazing!—his nails and teeth are still here.
He is a Buddha of the Age of Adornment,
a human antique, who has lasted a thousand years.
So much for artifacts of bronze or iron—
by now, *they* would have turned to dust!

For details of the remarkable practice of lacquer-mummification among the Chinese Buddhists, see Joseph Needham, Science and Civilisation in China, *vol. 5, part 2 (Cambridge, 1974), pp. 299ff.*

ROMANTIC SONG

Morning—I come by the avenue of vermilion
  gateways.
Evening—take my pleasure by bridges over green
  waters.
The house of songs—get a little drunk and stay
  ten days.
The dancing girls here—a thousand cash at a time!
This parrot, groggy with sleep, tries to speak;
this dappled horse, swift of foot, gallops without
  being whipped.
I'd rather spend one night with the goddess of Witch
  Mountain
than live on Mount Kou for a thousand years!

*Mount Kou was the site of the apotheosis of Prince Chin, who
took off on the back of a crane to become immortal.*

TWENTY-FIRST DAY of the Seventh Month

A memory returned to me and I wrote this down.

Foggy moon, birdcalls in the flowers at dawn,
in cold willow branches, orioles trembled on the
    edge of dream.
The words "Love Each Other" were written on
    the pillow,
and heavy incense curled from behind the curtains.

Her emotion had the lucidity of calm waters—
red color came to her cheeks as she smiled!
Back turned to the lamp, she changed her damp
    nightgown
and asked her lover to gather up her earrings.
Their tears of parting moistened the fragrant quilt,
tenderness of love, fragile as the wings of the cicada!

With silver tongs she stirred the ashes in the brazier
and traced these words: "As long as the sky . . ."
Lanterns hung from each story of the building;
the red railing of the balcony gave on the
    avenue below.

This was the scene of our love that year—
now I see only a tomb, overgrown with grass.
From the roots of the maples, I hear the whispering of
    a ghost
bearing the traces of her southern voice.
The stagnant clouds of this woman's soul
have been swept into rain
    over a mountain I do not know.

A WOMAN'S ROOM in Autumn

Autumn colors trickle through the gauze curtains;
cold fragrance floats in, bit by bit.
The chirping crickets rise from the dark walls;
fireflies flicker in the abandoned loom.
The bedroom fills with new moonlight;
frost on the bamboo screens—
    she changes to warmer clothes.
The migrating goose, the wanderer—
both are gone, only one
    will return.

PASSING THROUGH Suchou in the Rain

Out of a job, with roads to travel, still stuck here
    in Wu—
could it be this T'ao Ch'ien is a lazy pedant after all?
My soul seeks flowers, as if it were a butterfly,
or follows the waves in dreams, like a pelican.
A lonely lamp, skinny shadow—Cold Mountain
    Temple;
wild grass, flowing green—Hsia-chia Lake.
I've studied Tao, practiced Zen, and gotten nowhere:
now I'm like Yang Chu, who wouldn't give anyone
    a single hair off his head.

T'ao Ch'ien was the great Chin-dynasty poet who quit his job as a government official. Yang Chu was a philosopher of the mid-fourth century B.C. whose philosophy was misinterpreted as hedonism by some and selfishness by others.

PROSE BY
YÜAN HUNG-TAO

LETTER to Li Tzu-jan

Old Jan! Have you written any poems recently? If we don't write poems, how can we make it through these boring days? Human feelings demand some medium of expression—only then can we be happy. So some people do it through chess, some through sex, others through hobbies, and still others through writing. If the wise men of the past were a cut above ordinary people, it was simply because they had means for expressing their feelings; they weren't willing to go floating aimlessly through life.

I often see people who have no way to express their feelings. They run around busily all day long, as if they had lost something. They become depressed for no reason at all; they see beautiful sights and feel no joy. And they themselves can't understand why.

This is truly a living hell! Why speak of iron torture racks, bronze pillars, mountains of knife blades, or forests of swords? Oh, what a shame!

All in all, nothing in this world is *that* hard to do—just charge ahead and do it! A day will inevitably come when "the ditch will be dug and the waters flow through." For a man with talent like yours, there is nothing in the world that is impossible. I only fear that you will be overly cautious, that you may be unwilling to take the risk and plunge ahead. Well, force yourself a little! It would be a good idea not to prove yourself undeserving of a friend's encouragement.

NOTE WRITTEN After Chang Yu-Yü's Poem About Hui Mountain Stream

My friend Ch'iu Chang-ju of Ma-ch'eng traveled east to the Wu area, and then traveled back to T'uan-feng with thirty jars of water from Hui Mountain Stream. Chang-ju went ahead by himself, instructing his servants to follow behind with the jars suspended from shoulder-poles. The servants, annoyed by the weight of the water, spilled all of it into the Yangtze. When they reached Tao-kuan River, they refilled the jars with local mountain stream water.

Chang-ju, knowing nothing of this, boasted extravagantly about the water and invited a group of connoisseurs from the city to taste it. When they arrived on schedule, they sat in a circle in Chang-ju's studio with expressions of pleasant anticipation on their faces. A bottle was brought out, as well as porcelain cups, into which just a few drops of the water were poured. These were then passed around for everyone's comments, and then it was time to drink. The connoisseurs savored the water's bouquet for a while, and only then did they sip lightly and swallow, producing a gurgling sound in their throats. They looked at each other, sighed out loud, and said: "What superb water! Were it not for Chang-ju's exquisite taste, how could we ever have had the experience of drinking it in this lifetime!" They went on exclaiming in admiration without pause and then finally left for home.

Half a month later, the servants had an argument in the course of which the facts came out. Chang-ju was outraged and fired the servants involved. As for the connoisseurs who had drunk the water, when they heard about the matter they simply muttered a few embarrassed words.

My younger brother Hsiao-hsiu recently also went on a trip to the east and came back with jars of mountain stream water from Hui Mountain and Chung-leng. He wrote the names of the respective streams on red labels to record which jar came from which stream. When he returned home after a journey of over a month, the writing on the labels had worn off. I asked him: "Which came from Hui Mountain and which from Chung-leng? He couldn't tell. And even after drinking some water from each jar, he still couldn't tell. We looked at each other and roared with laughter.

But in actual fact, Hui Mountain water is far superior to water from Chung-leng, let alone Tao-kuan River! Since coming to the Wu area myself as a magistrate, I have tasted the waters many times and I am now able to distinguish among them. Reading the present poem by Yu-yü reminded me of these things that happened in the past, and before I knew it, I was doubled over with laughter! This affair was similar to the "appreciation of pork at Ho-yang" of which Su Tung-p'o wrote, so I have written about it to provide Yu-yü with a good laugh.

Chang Yu-yü probably refers to Chang Hsien-i, an authority on the I Ching (Book of Changes). Ch'iu Chang-ju was Yüan's friend Ch'iu T'an and Hsiao-hsiu was Yüan's younger brother Yüan Chung-tao.

DREAMS

Sitting at night in Pure Temple, I talked with my friend Fang and our conversation turned to the subject of strange dreams.

Fang said: "I once had a dream that was extremely bizarre. I came upon a district office with a vermilion gateway and guards holding elaborate halberds, as if it were a king's palace. I entered by way of the eastern staircase and noticed that in front of the main hall were two high towers with a ferocious-looking guard standing in each. These two men had red hair and green eyes—they were terrifying in appearance. On the central dais were standing three giants, several tens of feet tall, their bodies covered with strings of jewels. When I asked someone who they were, he answered: 'These are the demi-gods.' Next, I approached the dais, and one of the giants asked: 'Do you wish to observe your former life?' Beside me was a man in a black robe, who immediately led me out of the hall to the eastern corridor. There I saw a monk sitting on a reed mat, holding a wooden fish gong. His face was haggard and jaundiced, and his expression was one of depression and dissatisfaction.

"When I had finished looking at him, I was led back to the main hall, where the giant again questioned me: 'Do you wish to observe your next life?' Before he had finished speaking, a guard leaped down from one of the towers and brandished the iron cudgel he was holding above his head. Sparks flashed from it in all directions, and the giants and buildings all disappeared. Then the guard led me to a little hole, out of which he dragged a man whose neck was in fetters, whose hair was burned, and whose clothes were filthy. This, I realized, was myself. And so I began trying to imagine what evil deeds I had performed in my present life to merit such suffering, and then, weeping, I awoke."

Fang also said: "Once, when my late mother was still alive, I dreamed of a demon orderly who was holding a tally, similar to the ones used by attendants in our provincial and district offices. On it was inscribed my mother's name. It happened that a nephew on my sister's side was also present, and the two of us wept and pleaded with the demon: 'We desire to reduce our own allotted years to prolong mother's life!' The demon pointed to my nephew and said: 'How could a distaff relative be allowed to do this?' Jumping with excitement, I exclaimed: 'If that's so, you can subtract ten years from my life!' The demon orderly nodded yes and left. Exactly ten years later, my mother died."

With this, I said to Fang: "Your physiognomy is not that of a long-lived man, and your life span has been reduced by ten years. How many years could you have left? The time when you'll be wearing those fetters is drawing near!"

For a long time after this, Fang looked quite unhappy.

Fang was Fang Wen-tsun (d. 1609).

RECORDING Strange Events

I sat at night in Shuang-ch'ing Villa, trading recent ghost stories with T'ao Shih-k'uei.

Shih-k'uei said: "Last year my sister-in-law died. On the day of her death, one of our maidservants suddenly went crazy, saying that she was the wife of X from N village, that she had died of strangulation and had followed her fellow ghosts to this place to beg for food, and that as they were leaving, her way had been blocked by the masses of ghosts. Now she was famished and pleaded for a single grain of rice. As she beseeched us to give her food, her manner was pitiful and moving in the extreme. After a while, some cooked rice was brought. The girl fell flat on the ground and snapped out of it as if waking from sleep.

When we questioned her, she could not remember a thing."

T'ao also said: "In my home district, in the family of a certain scholar-official, the wife became ill. Suddenly she exclaimed that the girl X, or the young lady X, or the uncle X, or the nephew X had arrived. All of these were people who had been dead for one, two, or even ten years, and yet one was able to converse with them as if with living persons. After several days, the woman suddenly said that Yama had come to beat her. Immediately, she fell to the ground, writhing beneath the blows of the stick. Her screams of pain could be heard near and far, and all over her body there appeared welts, as if produced by a stick. Then she kneeled on the ground, motioning with her hands as if to ward off the stick—her ten fingers turned black and blue and started to drip blood. Next she began turning and twisting on her bed as quick as the wind. When someone questioned her, she said: 'Yama is grinding me!' The manifestations of her suffering were a hundred times more horrible than anything in ordinary life. After a few more days, she had recovered enough to claim that she had originally been an immortal in heaven who had been banished to this earth. She had forgotten her old life and had behaved enviously and jealously in this one, so she had been punished while still alive. Now that the punishment was over, she could return to heaven. When she had finished speaking, she died."

T'ao said further: "Recently, one of my cousin's grandsons, who had been married for less than six months, was visited night after night by a certain beautiful woman who would sleep with him.

Eventually she became his concubine. Before long, her actions became extremely strange, and she kept telling people that in this world there was nothing desirable, other than death—nothing else could bring her happiness. Several times she attempted to hang herself with her stocking laces or to throw herself into the water. Her people would stand around her and keep watch over her, but one night the person who was guarding her dozed off, and the woman killed herself by jumping down the toilet. This is quite similar to the affair of Li the Red."

These stories are all worth recording, so I have written them down here to expand the available accounts of strange matters.

T'ao Shih-k'uei was T'ao Wang-ling (1562–1609). Li the Red, a T'ang-dynasty poet who gave himself this name because he felt his poems were comparable to those of Li Po ("Li the White"), is said to have died by falling into a toilet, after which he was accorded the dubious distinction of being called the toilet demon. Yama is King of Hell in both Indian and Chinese tradition. For a good summary of modern anthropological interpretations of female possession, see I. M. Lewis, Ecstatic Religion (Harmondsworth, 1971).

Shao Mi: "Landscape with Figure, in the Manner of T'ang Yin." *Leaf from an album, ink and light colors on silk, 29.6 x 21.2 cm. National Palace Museum, Taipei.*

A LITTLE STORY About Living in the Mountains

A rich man who had suffered disappointment in a certain matter came to live at Ti Mountain for a while. He bowed to a recluse of that place and said: "To be as poor and ill as you are, sir, is something which anyone would hate, and yet your manner is as pleasant as the springtime, and your expression as clear as the moon after the rainclouds have disappeared. How strange!"

The recluse said: "There's nothing strange about it! Some time ago I vomited up blood and could not get out of bed for an entire year after that. The best doctors were unable to help me. I was sure that I would die and, in fact, it was rumored that I had already died. There was nothing I could do about it—I heard people speaking of my own death and, to my amazement, I got better! From this point of view, my present life is unexpected, and whatever comes to me in this life must be counted as unexpected gain. It is simple human nature that when one experiences unexpected gain, one cannot feel unhappy even if one tries."

The rich man said: "You live in obscurity here in the mountains. What could possibly happen to you that you would count as gain and feel happy about? This is stranger still!"

I said: "There's nothing strange about it! I keep in mind that in the recent past my two feet wouldn't hold me up, and now I can walk about—this is happiness! My arms could hardly move, and now I can paddle a boat—this is happiness! My waist and back could not support my weight, and now I can bend or lean as I please—this is happiness! Nor was I ever comfortable when lying down, and now I sleep soundly with peaceful snores—this is happiness! So, if you consider most people's desires and satisfactions to be happiness, then my unhappiness would be ten thousand times greater than yours. But if you consider my walking, standing, sitting, and lying down to be happiness, then you ought to be ten thousand times happier than me! What's so strange about that!"

The rich man said: "Nevertheless, you were ill and on the brink of death. It is for this reason that you developed your pleasant views. As for me, I have never been ill and never on the brink of death.

I said: "Since I am able to maintain the point of view of a man on the brink of death, even though I am actually *not* on the brink of death, why should you not be able to cultivate the point of view of a seriously ill man even though you are not ill?"

With this, the rich man finally realized what I was saying and, relaxing his expression and laughing out loud, he said: "Amazing! You are able to be happy and to make me happy too! Amazing!"

I said: "There's nothing amazing about it. The other day, I was walking below the city wall with a friend. We saw a beggar coming toward us, pleading mournfully. This beggar had a small head and face, delicate skin, a refined voice, and was walking slowly, as if each step was difficult. I assumed that this was a woman beggar, so I asked: 'Do you have a husband?' The beggar smiled faintly. I thought that perhaps the beggar did not understand the word 'husband,' so I asked: 'Do you have an old man?' The beggar smiled once again, as if slightly embarrassed. I said to my friend: 'Can it be that when romantic matters are brought up, even a beggar will be pleased?' At which the beggar said with a smile: 'I'm a man!' My friend and I realized that we had been wrong all along, so we laughed out loud, and the beggar laughed too."

I said: "You have come from far away—there are people who give you gruel, some who give you rice, and some who even give you money. In none of these cases do you forget that you are a beggar, so you never laugh. Now, just a moment ago when you laughed, did you feel that you were a beggar? When you forget that you are a beggar, you no longer *are* a beggar—you are the same as anyone else, the same as a rich man, the same as a nobleman with a fief of ten thousand households! Have I not given you something wonderful?'

"The beggar agreed, thanked me with a smile, and left.

"Now, if I can make a beggar happy, shouldn't I be

able to make a rich man like yourself happy? There's nothing amazing here!"

Such was the profundity of our conversation that the rich man forgot to leave. Mist encircled the darkening mountains; a temple bell sounded from the distant trees. I had already lent the man the use of my sleeping platform; now I tossed him the thick mat I had been sitting on as well.

He laughed and said: "I have heard that there are people who weep at night because they have no roofs over their heads. How could they ever get to stay in a warm house, with such a fine mat to sleep on?" Then he fell asleep.

When the speaker switches to the first person, it becomes clear that the recluse is Yüan himself.

MOUNT YANG

Mount Yang surges above all the surrounding mountains and connects with a range which extends over a distance of several tens of li. It falls under the jurisdiction of two subprefectures. Beneath the mountain is the Shrine of the White Dragon. According to the old people of the area, during the Eastern Chin dynasty (317–419), an elderly man wearing a white robe once stayed overnight at the house of a commoner and left the next day. The woman of the house became pregnant and later gave birth to a white dragon, complete with horns on its head. The dragon rose up into the sky and the woman was frightened to death.

Now, beneath he mountain, there is the Tomb of the Dragon's Mother, with a cypress tree in front of it that is some twenty spans in circumference. Several years ago, a white dragon was seen hanging from one of its branches like a bolt of silk, swaying back and forth and looking around as if trying to find its parents. Whenever there is a drought and the people here pray for rain, they are sure to be answered. Because of the magic power of the spot, it has been recorded in the official annals of ritual.

This year, in the sixth month, the drought demon acted up again, and Chiang Chin-chih and I accompanied the prefect when he prayed at the shrine. As he started, intense sunlight was glittering in the pool and not a sliver of cloud was to be seen anywhere in the sky. Chin-chih and I climbed to the summit, and just as we reached Arrow Tower, on all four sides clouds and fog arose from the mountains, forming a vast, gray mass in which one could not distinguish anything. Then, in the time it takes to inhale and exhale, rain poured down in torrents, filling the rice paddies with water. Chin-chih and I looked at each other in terror and left as quickly as we could.

Is it possible that dragons really are divine creatures?

Mount Yang is located northwest of Wu-hsien, near Great Lake (T'ai-hu) in Chiangsu Province. See Yüan's poem on Mount Yang, translated on page 69.

THE CAVE of the Jade City

The Jade City is over twenty li from the Five Waterfalls. The entrance to the cave is broad and the interior is at first like a huge mansion. After one has gone in a way, the path narrows slightly, then returns to its former breadth. Within the cave, rocks in the shapes of lotus flowers or human figures are numerous. There are three or four turnings, and then a hole that is so narrow that one can only get through by crawling. The two T'ao brothers and I went through flat on our bellies, lighting our way with torches. Smoke filled the available space, so that our tears fell like rain. Then I remembered hearing an old story about people suffocating because of torch smoke in caves; I became frightened and retreated, along with the T'aos. Only Wang Ching-hsü and an office clerk of Wu Subprefecture went ahead at the risk of their lives. They crossed four or five ridges, coming to the innermost depths of the cave, found their way blocked by a subterranean stream, and only then turned back.

SOLITARY MOUNTAIN

The recluse of Solitary Mountain had "a plum tree as his wife and cranes as his children." This was the highest man of leisure in the world! Such people as myself and my friends, precisely because we have wives and children, let ourselves in for all kinds of problems. We cannot get rid of them, and yet we are tired of being with them—it's like wearing a coat with tattered cotton padding and walking through a field of brambles and stickers that tug at your clothes with each step!

Recently, a man named Yü Seng-ju has taken up residence under Thunder Peak, and he too has no wife. Perhaps he is a reincarnation of the recluse of Solitary Mountain! He has written a group of poems on plum blossoms falling in the creek, and while I do not know how they might be felt to compare with the poetry of the recluse, he did turn out 150 of them in one night, which can certainly be called writing quickly! As for his practice of fasting and doing Zen meditation, this actually puts him a cut above the recluse.

Is there ever an age without remarkable men?

"The recluse of Solitary Mountain" was Lin Pu (967–1028), a major poet of the early Sung dynasty.

WEST LAKE and Shan-yin

. . . I once expressed the thought that West Lake is like a painting by one of the Sung-dynasty masters, and the scenery at Shan-yin is like a painting by one of the Yüan-dynasty masters. Flowers, birds, and human figures, all visible in every detail, rich and sparse areas, distant and near scenes, every color exquisitely fine: such is the scenery of West Lake. People without discernible features, trees without discernible branches, mountains without discernible vegetation, water without discernible ripples, everything abbreviated or suggested, the sense of distance arising from the forms: such is the scenery of Shan-yin. As to the question of which of the two is superior, I leave that to people possessed of a perceptive eye.

Shan-yin became famous in the Six Dynasties period, and became less popular starting with the T'ang. West Lake became known in the T'ang and is at its peak of popularity now. Perhaps scenic spots also undergo the vicissitudes of fate!

Chang Hung: *"Landscape in the Manner of Hsia Kuei."* Leaf from an album of landscapes after old masters, dated 1636, ink and colors on silk, 31.6 x 19.7 cm. Ching Yüan Chai Collection.

A RECORD OF LISTENING to the Rock of Echoing Waters

The rock is halfway up Heaven's Eye Mountain. If you listen to it quietly, the sound of flowing water can be heard from within, resonant and clear. Its name is the Rock of Echoing Waters. This rock is over twenty feet high, and twice this in breadth. It is strangely beautiful in its outer form and powerfully structured beneath the surface.

Let this serve to remedy the omission of this rock from rock catalogues of the past.

Heaven's Eye Mountain is located east of T'ai-hsien in Chiangsu Province.

EVEN-WITH-THE-CLOUDS

The Heavenly Gate of the mountain called Even-with-the-Clouds is a beautiful spot, but unfortunately the area below the cliff is cluttered up with inscriptions and epigraphs. How irritating! The people of Anhui just love to write graffiti; this is a shortcoming of theirs. And the officials who have held office there have been influenced by local custom. Even the small rocks are all covered with vermilion characters or plain engraved words. It's enough to make one gasp with anger!

I have noted that the law provides for standard punishments for those who plunder the mountains or dig illegal mine shafts. Why is it that vulgar scholar-officials can desecrate the Mountain Spirit with impunity? Buddhism says that all evil action will lead to appropriate retribution. The acts I am describing are in a class with murder and robbery, and yet Buddhism makes no mention of them. This is an oversight on the part of the canon.

What crimes have the green mountains and white rocks ever committed, that their faces should be branded and their skin cut? Oh, how inhumane!

The rocks at the Peaks of the Five Elders are all beautiful but slightly lacking in rich luster. Also, the mountain forms themselves are not that spectacular, so visitors need not stay too long. If the Taoist shrines would reduce the number of their rooms, then officials would come here less frequently. Eventually, the inscriptions would become effaced, lichens would cover the rocks, and, unless the god of this mountain is totally lacking in spiritual efficacy, in less than one hundred or so years, Even-with-the-Clouds should return to its pristine beauty.

My fellow travelers were Mei Chi-pao, T'ao Chou-wang, P'an Ching-shen, Fang Tzu-kung, the monk Pi-hui, and the two gentlemen Chang and Li. We stayed for five nights, then continued traveling.

For the phrase "rocks at the Peaks of the Five Elders . . . ," an alternative version of the text has been partially followed.

A RECORD OF STAYING OVERNIGHT at the Terrace of Falling Stones

After coming down from Even-with-the-Clouds, we took a raft downstream to the Terrace of Falling

Stones. Here, stones have fallen along the bank of the stream, creating a cliff on top of which one could spread out a mat. The monks living on shore were not friendly, and when they heard that some travelers had arrived, they closed the doors to their chambers.

The building closest to the nearby mountain was very picturesque, so I said to Shih-k'uei: "Let's just barge in! Who needs to ask the monks?' I dragged Shih-k'uei in with me, and the others followed timidly. The sunlight glittering on the stream and the blue-green colors of the mountain seemed to reflect off the tables and benches.

Two youths then appeared and bowed to us. They had expressions of serenity on their faces. Indicating Shih-k'uei, one of our group said: "This is the venerable T'ao of K'uai-chi." The youths immediately jumped to attention, bowed, and went to set out some wine for us in the pavilion. We discussed the life of an examination candidate with them until midnight. The sound of the stream penetrated the night like the wind in ten thousand pines.

The next morning, the youths asked us for poems and plaque inscriptions. I named the pavilion "Stream Sound." Shih-k'uei said: "This is the rain I dreamed of at Heaven's Eye!" So I named the studio "Dreaming of Rain." We each wrote two poems for the occasion and gave them to the youths.

A RECORD OF A TRIP to Ch'ung-kuo Temple

It was the year *chi-hai* [1599], the third day of the third month. It had been decided that Po-hsiu, Chao-su, Sheng-po, and myself would celebrate the customary day of purification beside the river beyond the west gate of the city, but because a sandstorm started up, we took shelter in Ch'ung-kuo Temple.

As it happened, Wang Chang-fu and my younger brother were having a literary gathering at this very place, so we all got drunk together and had smiles on our faces the whole day. Everyone agreed that this was our first real intoxication since the beginning of spring.

One of the temple monks then led us to see the image of Tutor Yao. Yao was dignified and imposing, and his eyes seemed to flash like lightning. The inscription consisted of the words: "My true nature is that of a monk," written out by the Tutor in his own calligraphy.

Next, we visited the hostel for foreign monks, and here we saw images of Manjushri and other figures.

One had a blue face and the head of a boar; it was fat and dwarfish, wore human heads all over its body, had sixteen legs arranged in parallel fashion, and held many kinds of weapons. This image was extremely ferocious in appearance. The monk explained that it had been presented by the Tibetans, who brought many images of this kind, and he also told us about the customs of Tibet and how far away it was. In sum, it can be said that the provinces of Tibet consider even the lowest grade of Chinese tea to be a national treasure and use it as a medium of exchange. Gold and silver, strangely enough, are not in circulation. The country is without rice paddies, and the people eat only wheat and pulse. There is a local overlord for every several tens of li, something like the administrative system of China. But it is a backward, impoverished country.

At this point, Po-hsiu and Chao-su left because they had official duties to attend to the following morning, The rest of us talked about the *I Ching* [Book of Changes] until midnight. New points of discussion kept coming up as we talked, and we did not want to leave but, as our servants had been waiting a long time in the cold night, we had no choice but to go.

Tutor Yao was Yao Kuang-hsiao (1335–1418), who became a monk at the age of fourteen, but resumed a lay name when appointed Tutor to the Heir Apparent. He was a poet and a painter, as well as one of the most influential political advisors of his day.

FROM "FIELDS OF INK: Miscellaneous Notes"

On a certain day, I went to the Office of Tribute

Inspections, where I met an envoy from Annam. The tribute he had brought consisted of gold and silver vessels, which were embellished with rather unskilled designs. Aside from this, he had only brought a little sandalwood, laka-wood, and ivory.

I asked this envoy whether he could do calligraphy, and he said: "I can." So I gave him a brush, and he wrote out a quatrain in cursive script [ts'ao-shu]:

> The path meanders over a stone bridge,
>> the stream bends nine times;
> the clouds veil an embankment of bamboo
>> groves
>> with three little houses.
> The gates are half closed,
>> wildflowers are falling;
> one cry from a bird—a calm day in spring.

His cursive was virtually impossible to read, so I asked him to write the standard forms beside each character, and these were no different from the ones used here in China.

The Annamese (Vietnamese), like the Koreans and Japanese, wrote much of their poetry in Chinese, partly because they admired Chinese culture and wished to emulate it, and partly because this ability proved useful in dealing with Chinese diplomats and officials.

A BIOGRAPHY of the Old Drunkard

The Old Drunkard—no one knows where he comes from. Nor has he told anyone his name. Since he's always drunk, I call him the Old Drunkard. Each year he travels between north and south China. He wears a seven-brim hat and embroidered robes; he has high cheekbones and a broad jawbone. His beard hangs down to his belly—to look at him, you'd think he was a ferocious general. He is perhaps fifty years old or so, but has no companions or followers. In his hand he carries a yellow bamboo basket. He spends the entire day dead drunk and seems asleep even in broad daylight. The stench of his boozy breath can be smelled a hundred paces away. He walks the streets looking for wine and, in a short while, he has drunk at over ten wine shops!—yet he seems no drunker than before.

The Old Drunkard does not eat a grain diet; he eats only centipedes, spiders, toads, and any sort of insect. The children in town are terrified of him—they grab whatever vermin they can find and offer these to him to eat. Wherever he walks, over one hundred people can always be seen trailing after him and staring. If anyone insults him, he rattles off a few words, some of which inevitably touch upon an intimate secret of the person, who then runs away in fright.

In his basket, the Old Drunkard always carries several tens of dried centipedes. If asked why, he says: "When it's cold, you can still get wine, but you can't get any of these."

When Po-hsiu told me about this man, I thought the whole thing was an exaggeration, so I invited him to my house for a drink. The boy servant found more than ten verminous insects and offered them to him. He swallowed all of them alive! Each little bug he would dip in his wine cup, as one dips chicken in vinegar, and then he would wash them down with wine. As for the centipedes, which were five or six inches long, he would pick up each one with cedar needles, remove their pincers, then place them, still alive, in his mouth. The red legs could be seen moving frantically between his whiskered lips: all of us got goose flesh just watching! But the Old Drunkard was obviously enjoying himself, chewing away with relish, as if he were dining upon essence of bear or suckling pig. When he was asked which delicacies were his favorite, he replied: "Scorpions taste wonderful, but unfortunately you can't get them down south. Centipedes are second best, and of the spiders, I prefer small ones. But you shouldn't eat too many ants, because they'll make you depressed." Then I asked what benefit he derived from his diet, and he said: "None! I do it just for fun!"

After this, the Old Drunkard and I became quite close. Whenever he came, he would crouch down on the stairs, call for wine, and drink away. If anyone treated him like an honored guest, he would immediately show his displeasure. He talked on and on about many strange subjects. Every so often, something he said would be truly mysterious, but he would not answer any inquiries about it, and if I repeatedly questioned him, he would purposely change the subject.

One day I went out with my uncles, and we were speaking about the beautiful sights at Gold Mountain and Mount Chiao, when we met the old drunkard along the road. My second uncle mentioned that in a certain year he had climbed Gold Mountain. The Old Drunkard smiled and said: "Could it be that the military advisor so-and-so was host, and the secretary so-and-so also went along?" My uncle was astonished, but when the Old Drunkard was asked how he had come to know these things, he did not answer. At a later time, someone managed to take a quick look into his basket and saw something like a certificate of official appointment in it. He claimed that the Old Drunkard had been a well-endowed official in the area, which seemed to make sense.

The Old Drunkard's behavior was truly bizarre. He had no fixed home. At night he would stay at an old shrine of beneath the eaves of the city gates. He was constantly repeating the words: "All dharmas return to the One—where does the One return?" whether moving about, staying in one place, sitting, sleeping, or conversing. If anyone asked him why, he would not answer.

Once when I was on my way to an official post, I saw him again at Sha-shih, but I do not know where he is now.

Shih-kung says: I often see strange people in the

cities and regret that I know nothing about their lives. And I regret that of the strange people holed up in the forests and mountains, probably only one out of ten appears in the cities! As for the strange people recorded in the official records and unofficial books, surely they represent no more than one tenth of those who do appear in the cities. Since these are people with no ambition to become known, and since they associate only with butchers, wine merchants, shop owners, wandering monks, and beggars, how many worthy scholar-officials even get to know about them and hand down their stories? In the past, I have heard of a woman known as the Cap-wearing Immortal, and a Taoist of the Single Gourd, both living in Feng-chou. Recently, several people in the Wu-han area have been acting quite strange, and one of them seems to know a thing or two about the Tao. Yes, it appears that this is what is meant by the old saying: "Though he possesses the powers of a dragon, he remains hidden."

Shih-kung was one of Yüan's names. "Though he possesses . . ." is a quotation from the "Wen-yen," one of the appendices to the I Ching. This passage occurs in the commentary to the first line of the first hexagram, ch'ien.

Inklings Editions are a production of Weather-hill, Inc., publishers of fine books on Asia and the Pacific. Supervising editor: Margaret E. Taylor. Book design and typography: Liz Trovato. Production supervision: Bill Rose. Text composition: G & H Soho, Inc., Hoboken, New Jersey. Printing and binding: Daamen, Inc., West Rutland, Vermont. The typeface used is Berkely Old Style.